My Life with Suzuki

by

Waltraud Suzuki

My Life with Suzuki

by

Waltraud Suzuki

Suzuki Method International
Summy-Birchard, Inc.
Exclusive print rights administered by
Alfred Music Publishing Co., Inc.

Suzuki Method International

Introduction

by

Henry Turner

I first met Waltraud Suzuki in 1979, at the International Suzuki Conference, which was held in Munich that year. Plans to set up the British Suzuki Institute were already far advanced, and Felicity Lipman and my wife, Anne Turner, who subsequently became musical directors of the Institute, had been invited to attend.

Dr. and Mrs. Suzuki paid their first visit to England later that year and my wife and I were honoured to be able to act as their hosts on that occasion, and again on their subsequent trips to Europe.

On that first visit, I well remember that Waltraud arrived with a large and imposing suitcase, which contained not only all her own things, but also all Dr. Suzuki's clothes, and we were immediately faced with a crisis. No one could remember the combination of the lock, and the suitcase remained obstinately closed. In desperation, my aid was sought. I gazed at the suitcase, and twiddled the numbers on the lock; and to my surprise and relief, the suitcase opened. I had rendered my first service to the Suzuki movement, and acquired a totally undeserved reputation as handyman!

Anne and I are among those who have been urging Waltraud to write down the story of her meeting with the young Shinichi Suzuki, and their life together, and I am delighted to be able to introduce what I am sure you will agree is a fascinating account of nearly six decades of shared experiences.

And what a story it is! Those of us who have the privilege of knowing her will recognize Waltraud's voice telling us of a young woman moving from the familiar cultivated surroundings of mid-twenties Berlin to the totally unfamiliar atmosphere of pre-war Japan; the horrors and deprivations of the war years; and the frustration and disorientation of the immediate postwar years. And through it all, the indomitable courage with which she supported Dr. Suzuki in his efforts to establish his educational theories, and to build up the Talent Education Institute.

To revert to the analogy of the suitcase; in a very real sense it was Waltraud's never-failing support which made it possible to unlock the treasure-chest of Dr. Suzuki's teaching: not by any fortunate accident, but by love, sheer courage, and single-minded determination over many years.

Although, with characteristic modesty Waltraud would probably play down her role, I think the following pages make it clear how much the thousands of children, parents and teachers around the world whose lives have been enriched by Dr. Suzuki owe to the selfless support he has received from his wife.

Preface

People who have known me for some years all say: "You should write a book".

Well, I am not one of the gifted authors who can successfully intermingle fantasy and reality, but in a very plain way I have tried to write down some of my life's reminiscences.

It is not my intention to discuss Suzuki's philosophy and work in detail in this book, since those subjects are sufficiently covered in *Nurtured by Love, Ability Development from Age Zero,* and many other publications about Suzuki.

This is just an account of our life together.

Waltraud Suzuki

My grateful thanks to
Henry and Anne Turner
who encouraged me to
finally write this book.

Contents

Chapter 1

Growing up During the First World War

I was born in 1905 in Berlin, Germany into an upper middle class family as the third and last child. There followed a happy childhood, except for the piano lessons my sister and I had to attend from the age of six, and my mother's summons when visitors came, "Now play a little for the guests". I didn't like that at all. The conventional lessons did not inspire me, but no Talent Education or Suzuki Method existed then.

At that time, I didn't know what life held in store for me, and fate goes curious ways.

In 1914, the First World War started. Two years later my father died after a prolonged illness. Those years were very hard. Food was scarce. I went to school without breakfast and when I came home from school there was no lunch. I went down to the greengrocers to relieve my mother who had been standing there in line since early morning in hopes of getting some (frozen) potatoes. My sister and I shared this task. Sometimes, when my turn came, everything was sold out. There was not enough food for the ration cards.

The year 1917 was called the rutabaga year, since there was hardly anything else to eat, no fat or potatoes, let alone meat to make them more appetizing. Bread, like everything else, was rationed. There too, one had to stand in line for hours to receive one loaf. It was still hot when it was sold, direct from the oven, baked only once a week. One could compress the loaf in one hand. Little blades of straw and what not could be found in the slices; but it was something to eat. My mother grieved very much on our behalf, but we always said cheerfully, "We are not hungry". It seems to me children take everything in their stride, and are still happy.

In 1918 the war ended; but what an end!!! The monarchy was gone, there was confusion, revolution and strikes. Armored trucks were roaming the streets of Berlin. All of a sudden the riders would shout, "Clear the street!" and start shooting for whatever reason at all. Passers-by would press themselves against house walls until the crazy incident was over. Years later one could occasionally see battered and ragged soldiers returning from the front.

Revolution in Berlin

Then followed the run-away inflation. My mother could not cope anymore with the constantly rising prices. If something cost 100,000 marks in the morning, it cost 150,000 or 200,000 marks in the afternoon. No nation in the world except Germany has ever experienced such crazy inflation. (Nothing to be proud of!) Finally, one loaf of bread cost one million marks. After millions, we had to count in billions and trillions.

No one, especially older people, could count anymore. Overnight there was the Renten-mark. Suddenly one mark was one mark again, but with the exception of the blackmarketeers, almost everyone was poor overnight.

Chapter 2

The Post-War Years— Meeting with Suzuki

At that time, my brother had founded a small orchestra and was supporting our family. I had taken up my long-interrupted piano studies and voice lessons at the Stern'sche Conservatory. I liked singing much more than piano playing.

We still lived in a rather big apartment. There was a family meeting to decide if we should move to a smaller one or take in lodgers. We opted for the latter, because even though there was little money, we did not want to leave our comfortable home for smaller surroundings. And where we were, we could still have our little "home concerts". My brother played the violin, my sister the piano and I sang. At that time in Berlin, this was still the normal way to live for many people, ignoring all the upheavals and materialism outside.

Berlin, 1924
My brother, sister, and I at home

On one such occasion at a home of friends, I met a violin student — Shinichi Suzuki.

Shinichi Suzuki, c. 1924

Waltraud, c. 1924

Since I was alone, he asked whether he could accompany me home, which offer I gratefully accepted. He said he would like to meet my family, and I told him my father was deceased, but he was welcome to meet my mother, brother and sister.

Suzuki came the very next day, and then nearly every day.

My Mother, Sophie (1878-1976)

My Brother, Albert (1901-1941)

My Sister, Erna (1902-   )

We went to concerts together, listened to Kreisler and many other wonderful soloists with the outstanding conductors of the Philharmonic orchestra —Furtwängler and Bruno Walter. Another wonderful artist was Arthur Schnabel, whose interpretations of all of Beethoven's sonatas are also unforgettable.

And there were the chamber music evenings at the Singakademie. We seldom missed a performance of the Busch Quartet, but *never* missed the Klingler Quartet. Berlin was at her cultural zenith. All those great musicians we heard are gone by now.

Then, of course, there were the home concerts at different families' homes: Einstein, Klingler and not so famous ones.

Albert Einstein
(Translation of Inscription:
To Mr. Shinichi Suzuki with kind memories
Albert Einstein, Nov. 1926)

At our concerts at home, when my brother was busy, Shinichi would accompany my sister and myself on his violin. One of his younger brothers came from Japan to study cello in Leipzig. Of course, we met him and found him also very nice. We wondered whether all Japanese were as wonderful as these two brothers. Now, of course, I know that Shinichi Suzuki is a very special human being, and believe there are only very, very few in the whole world like him. His whole life is dedicated to serving others. Those who have met him will agree with me.

After five years of close association, Shinichi and I got very attached to each other, and decided to get married, since we were certain we could not live without each other.

Sixty years ago in Germany one had a very hazy idea about Japan. Shinichi said, "We will live in Switzerland, you cannot live in Japan". I answered, "Why not? You live there". When Suzuki informed his father of our wedding plans, Mr. Suzuki sent his eldest son to have a look at our family. Naturally, he gave another reason for coming. His report must have been favourable, because there were no objections. But from my side — oh dear! Not from my immediate family, they all loved Shinichi. But when our engagement was announced, my mother's relatives came nearly every day to reproach her, "How can you allow Waltraud to marry a Japanese? How can you let her go to such a far away country which nobody knows anything about? etc. etc.". "And no one will come to the wedding". They were all there!

Chapter 3

The Wedding

It was a beautiful wedding. The big church was filled to capacity. I was known to the parish, because every Sunday and on holidays I used to sing in the choir and also the solo parts in masses by Vivaldi, and orchestra masses by Mozart, Schubert, *etc.*

In Germany, unlike the United States, the groom comes to the church with the bride. We arrived in a bridal carriage pulled by white horses and attended by two coachmen in livery—one standing on a footboard at the back. The church bells started ringing before we even arrived at the door and a red carpet was rolled out from the altar, down the aisle, right out to the carriage. Two little children walked along the carpet in front of us, strewing flowers. The organ was playing and the choir was singing.

After the ceremony, as we walked back out to the bridal carriage, a choir member played *Ave Maria* on the violin, accompanied by the organ.

The Wedding
February 8, 1928

Suzuki often went to church without my knowing it, and became a Catholic long before we married.

Chapter 4

From Berlin to Nagoya

We had been married only for about four months when a cable came asking us to come to Japan as soon as possible because Shinichi's mother was critically ill. We went by train via Siberia. It would have taken much longer by ship and there were no airplanes like today.

Suzuki's Mother, Ryoh.

Suzuki's Father, Masakichi.

We finally arrived in Nagoya, Suzuki's birthplace and the third largest city in Japan.   Since World War II it has been very nicely built up, but at that time, coming as I did directly from Berlin, I thought it was a village.

The whole family, except Shinichi's mother and father, but including all the maids, was at the station to welcome us.   And REPORTERS!!!   I am used to them now, but at that time I was terribly shy and felt dreadful as they took photos and photos and more photos.   I was glad when we arrived at the house.   Since I did not know one word of Japanese, I just tried to smile at everyone, not knowing who was who.

Shinichi's mother was lying down but tried to sit up to welcome us, despite her obvious pain.   I was distressed that I could not talk to her or make her comfortable in any way.

**Shinichi's father lived in a big comfortable
house with a billiard room attached. The
Japanese garden was beautifully landscaped.**

Shinichi and I had the use of a small house across
from my parents-in-law. When I first saw it I was
completely puzzled: there was no furniture at all! The
Japanese measure the size of their rooms in terms of tatami,
special rice-straw mats measuring 1.8 meters long by 90
centimeters wide. We had one very big room—a 50-tatami
room—with beautiful flower arrangements and other decorations in the alcoves. There were smaller rooms, too,
and none had any furniture.

Now I can see that the Japanese lifestyle is very prac-
tical. They don't need as many rooms in their houses as we
do in the Western World. One room can serve as a bedroom
(the bedding is rolled up and stored out of sight during the
day), but it can also serve as a dining room and/or a living
room. The diners sit on floor cushions and eat from a knee-
high table. This same table can be used for writing.

If overnight guests show up—no problem. The bedding will just be put out in one of the rooms. There is no need
for a guest room.

I can see all that now, but just after my arrival I wanted a *chair!* We went to what was the only department store in Nagoya at that time and bought a rattan set—a sofa, two chairs, and a table. It looked awfully forlorn in the big room, so I had it moved into the small one. There I spent most of my time.

There were no windows in the room, just sliding glass doors all around. One beautiful day I had those doors open and was embroidering a tablecloth. Something made me glance up and I was PETRIFIED! A large snake, her head high and her tongue flicking in and out, was in the doorway and moving into the room!

After the initial shock I screamed and ran from the room. Shinichi and his younger brother, and all the maids, came running. When I told my husband what had frightened me and he, in turn, had explained it to the others, they all went into the room to shoo the snake back into the garden.

Sitting in my ratan chair in my
new home in Nagoya.

**In the garden.
Our 2 dogs are playing by my feet.**

Outside my brother-in-law's house.

One of Shinichi's brothers lived with his family in a beautiful Western-style house right across the street from us on a small hill. My father-in-law wanted to build a house for us there too. The timber was already on the site, but I didn't want to live in Nagoya. Shinichi's father owned a furniture factory as well as the violin factory, and our dining room set, which I still use today, was built there. It is beautiful.

Not long after our arrival, there was a welcoming party in a hotel, where I was introduced as a new member of the Suzuki clan. Later on there was another Japanese-style, gathering, with everyone sitting on the floor. As a result, half-way through the seemingly endless dinner party I couldn't feel my legs anymore. My legs were useless at the moment, but I couldn't stand the pain any longer. So I slowly opened the *shoji* (sliding paper door) behind me, and slid with the cushion on which I sat, into the hallway, and closed the door. I thought I was unobserved, but no such luck. Many came running wanting to help me, but I still couldn't get up and just sat there.

My first New Year celebration in Japan was a nightmare. The maids were busy for days preparing special, different New Year's food, and packed it in beautiful lacquer boxes. Very nice to look at. But then, from January first to the 15th there came those lacquer boxes on the table with all the strange food. Nowadays all this has changed, but in the old days it was customary to prepare all the food in advance to ensure having only a little bit of work to do through the New Year's festival.

My father-in-law owned a chauffeur-driven Packard, and told me I could use it exclusively once a week. I was delighted but soon had to give up my excursions. Wherever I went, people stared at me as soon as I left the car. (It's a feeling that makes one sympathize with a monkey in a zoo.)

Father Suzuki's Packard Automobile

One time when I was looking at the displays in a department store, I turned around, and couldn't move, because a wall of people was surrounding me. They were all whispering to each other. Of course, I didn't understand anything, and was greatly shocked, but I caught the one word, *kirei*, repeated over and over again. I later asked my husband about it and he said it meant "pretty" or "beautiful". This admiration should have made me feel good, but instead I felt very uncomfortable and was too timid to leave the house. I just walked around in the garden.

Once when I was sitting on the step of the teahouse admiring the cherry blossoms, I heard whispering again.

Looking around, I saw a group of schoolgirls hanging over the fence looking at me. That was enough for me! I told my husband I wanted to move to Tokyo where there were more foreigners and I wouldn't be such a novelty.

The tea house is on the left, not visible in this photo.

Shortly after our arrival in Nagoya, I wanted a teacher so I could learn a language like that. My husband said, "Why do you want to learn a language like that? Only the Japanese speak it, and we will not stay here. We will live in Switzerland". (I wonder whether Talent Education or the Suzuki method with the "mother tongue" approach would have been borne had we moved to Switzerland at that time?)

We went to church every Sunday where there was an elderly German priest. The family may have wondered that we visited the church every Sunday, but no one interfered. Later in Matsumoto, Shinichi's two sisters and his younger brother and their families all became Catholics.

During the year we lived in Nagoya, my mother-in-law died. Then, Shinichi's father, who owned a furniture factory and a violin factory told the family that he had lost all his money in New York's 'Black Friday'. If he had only economized right away instead of borrowing money from loan sharks, his situation wouldn't have been too bad, because he owned plenty of land and houses. He owned a whole street, named 'Suzuki street'. But the Suzukis are very impractical, and went on living in the style they were accustomed to before the father's declaration.

My fondest memories of Nagoya are the visits to Marquis Tokugawa's beautiful mansion, where he acquainted me with different Japanese arts, such has *Noh, etc.*. The artists performed on a huge stage. I found it fascinating, beautiful and strange.

Chapter 5

We Move to Tokyo

In Tokyo, we were soon accepted in the foreign and Japanese music circles and society. But we were poor. It was difficult for me to reciprocate all the cocktail and dinner invitations. Sometimes I couldn't even pay our gas bill. And my husband was and never has been concerned with money. Unlike my own experience through the First World War, for him money had always been there. So, he still always took taxis where ever he went. Once he came home and said, "Please give me one yen, I have to pay the taxi and have no money". A yen at that time had some value. There was another coin — *go rin* — worth half a yen. And for a *go rin*, one could buy half a chicken. When Shinichi had paid the taxi, I told him, "That was our last yen. I don't know what we will eat tomorrow". But my husband found this very amusing and laughed. Then he went to his brother to borrow some money.

We still received living expenses from my father-in-law, and I didn't like it, and told my husband that he had to earn our own livelihood. Shinichi had sold his beautiful Vuillaume violin to help his father. My Bechstein grand piano had arrived from Germany. Shinichi told me his father had asked him whether I would sell it to pay his debts. At that time, there were very few such instruments in Japan, and they were very valuable. Of course, losing my Bechstein made me sad, but I asked myself how I would feel if I asked my husband to do something for *my* family and he refused. So I said: "Yes, if it really helps".

Shinichi had earlier given successful concerts, but didn't like it, saying there were better artists than he who could do that. Chamber music was rare in Japan. So he

founded the Suzuki Quartet with his brothers in 1929. They
were excellent, and traveled around Japan giving concerts.

The Suzuki Quartet
Shinichi, 1st Violin; Kikuo, 2nd Violin;
Fumiyo, Cello; Akira, Viola.

Unfortunately all their recordings were lost during
the war. Suzuki also started teaching at the Imperial and
Kunitachi Conservatories.

The Suzuki Trio
Shinichi, Fumiyo and Prof. Leo Sirota.

During the summer, at vacation time, we rented a little cottage in Kutsukake, now Naka-Karuizawa, to escape the hot, humid climate in Tokyo. The Marquis Tokugawa, whom I had met in Nagoya and who taught me to appreciate so much about Japanese culture, had a villa in Karuizawa, and we visited each other. Our families visited each other and had a lovely time.

In Karuizawa (trying on a kimono).

Around 1930 the father of four-year-old Toshiya Eto brought him to Suzuki for violin lessons. Shinichi wondered how on earth he could teach such a small child. Soon after Eto, Koji Toyoda, not quite three years old, came. So it started. More and more little ones came. Our house was like a kindergarten. Shinichi worked out manuals which embodied techniques, step by step, increasing in difficulty, but without etudes, which children don't like too much. But they liked the 'songs' and did not notice the increasingly difficult techniques. Today, those ten manuals are as appropriate as before. It took Suzuki ten years to develop and complete them in this form.

My mother and sister visit us in Tokyo

My mother and sister came to visit us in Tokyo. It was wonderful to see them again and show them around. Not too long after their return, my brother contracted influenza with a high fever and died rather young. I had always secretly hoped that he would come to Japan.

With us, all went well for a few years. We had now rented a little house all year round on Lake Ashiya, Hakone, where Suzuki liked to fish. We now spent all vacation time there, except in winter, when we went skiing.

Skiing in Sugadaira.

The Zeppelin over Tokyo.
"It felt like greetings from home."

The Luftschiff 'Zeppelin' came from Germany for a visit. The hour of the Zeppelin's flying over Tokyo was announced, and the streets were full of people who wanted to have a look at this strange flying object which they had never seen before. They were amazed. For me it was like a greeting from my home country, and a nostalgic sight.

Chapter 6

The War Years in Japan

Then the second World War came as a shock and ended our placid life. After some time I urged Shinichi to evacuate as most of our acquaintances had done already. So finally, when the music schools closed he said I should go to the Hakone cottage, while he would go to Kiso-Fukushima to help the Nagoya Violin Factory, part of which had moved there. So we parted, thinking the war would not last long. Most foreigners went to Karuizawa or Hakone. The latter was like a German village. Naturally, there were food rations. The leader of the Germans in Hakone told me I should get the Japanese rations. (I was a member of the German Club). The Japanese side said I should get the German ones. Finally, I received the German rations—a few potatoes, once in a while a little bread, *etc.* Rice was strictly for the Japanese. We seldom got vegetables or fruits. But once I got an apple. I treasured and kept it for Shinichi's next visit. He was so pleased, and I urged him to eat it; but he said he would enjoy it later. Of course he did not eat it, but took it along to give it to his nephews. At this time he lived with his widowed sister and her two boys. I had rented a tiny bit of land, two meters square, to grow some vegetables. We received some seeds with our rations. Tomatoes and cucumbers came along nicely. Then one night there was a typhoon and the next morning everything was gone. But I was lucky and was able to grow one cabbage. What a feast, even without anything else except salt.

The food situation grew worse. The German sailors from submarines, called blockade-runners, got two weeks vacation in Hakone, and they provided the German community with whatever they captured from American ships. Once the booty was only green coffee beans. We roasted the beans in the frying pan, and the coffee smell all over Hakone was delicious.   But, after all, black coffee alone doesn't fill the stomach.

The war dragged on and on.   Hakone is rather cold in winter and I had nothing with which to heat my little house.   One day while I was walking briskly up and down the street just to keep warm some German sailors asked me why I didn't stay near my warm stove in such weather.   I told them I had nothing with which to heat the stove and they offered to bring me some wood.   When I asked where they would find it they said that on the other side of the lake plenty of wood was just lying about, rotting on the ground.   So they rowed across the lake and actually brought me boatloads of wood!   I was very happy because even if I didn't have enough to eat, at least I would be warm.

But no sooner had the last twig been brought inside than the mayor of Hakone came with ominous stories about how I would be jailed since, apparently, my "helpful" sailors had purloined the Imperial wood!

I was furious.   This man had seen the sailors hauling the wood, so why hadn't he stopped them?   Why had he waited till it was unloaded?   I asked him how I was supposed to transport it back?   Besides, how was I supposed to know it was Imperial wood since there was no chrysanthemum (the Emperor's coat of arms) on it.

Of course, this made the mayor furious, too, and he left my house with the flat order, "Return it at once—or else"! Having no choice I went out looking for the sailors.   When I found one I recognized I told him what had happened and begged him and his companions to return the wood to where they had found it.   So then THEY were angry, but they did return all the wood.

The next day some of the German women asked me where my halo was.   I had no idea what they were talking about till they laughed and said, "Oh, you touched Imperial wood"! Apparently the angry sailors had spread the story throughout the German community in Hakone.

But some good did come of the incident. We were allocated woodcutters, recruited from the German men still living in Tokyo and Yokohama. Since I had created the incident with the Imperial wood, I was the first person to get a woodcutter (lodged in my home).

I protested to the German leader, "How can I have a strange man in this tiny house with me? Look at it—only two rooms, a three-tatami one and a six-tatami one, separated only by paper doors". But no matter how I protested, it was to no avail.

The German leader just said, "You are married and he is married. If you refuse to house him, your food rations will be cut off".

How helpless I felt in the face of such force. Then it dawned on me that the people in Germany were equally helpless against this hateful Nazi regime.

I'm happy to say I survived the two weeks with the woodcutter, a very quiet man. I gave him my bed in the three-tatami room and moved my self into the kitchen, where I slept on the wooden floor.

But there were a number of Japanese who weren't much better than the Germans. It had been unofficially decided that everyone should dress very simply as some sort of gesture of support for the war effort. The Japanese women wore *mompei*, a kind of baggy pants over their kimonos. One day when I was feeling almost overwhelmed by all the problems of the war I tried to cheer myself up by wearing a nice dress and a string of pearls. I started off for a walk, but I didn't get far.

From his station in the center of the intersection a policeman shouted, "Suzuki-san, don't you know there's a war on"?

"Of course I know that", I replied.

"Then why do you dress up like that"? he shouted back.

Had he spoken politely and not shouted at me, I might have responded civilly. As it was, I retorted, "If you tell me that Japan will win the war if I go around in sackcloth, then MAYBE I will do it"! I returned to my house more depressed than ever.

Another little encounter with police happened, when my shoes badly needed new soles. I asked a German lady whether she knew of someone in Hakone who could repair them. She pointed to a little house occupied by a white Russian who could do the job. I picked up my shoes and went over there. We communicated in Japanese.

When I left his house there was a policeman standing there who asked, "What did you do in there"?

I told him I had brought my shoes to be repaired.

He shouted, "Don't you know you are not allowed to talk to him"?

Well, I didn't know that in the first place, but answered, "If YOU will repair my shoes, I won't have to go to him", and left him standing there.

All those incidents (there were more) did not increase my love for the Japanese. The ones I met THEN seemed to be of a different breed from those I had encountered in all the years of living in Japan. But worse was to come.

One day a man from the dreaded *Kempeitai*, the secret Japanese police, came into my house.

"You are a Japanese citizen", he said. I answered that I knew that.

He continued, "You are always speaking with the German people; you will tell us everything they are talking about".

Furiously I said, "I am not spying for you. If you want to know something, find it out yourself. Get out"!

He didn't and I shouted again, "GET OUT". Since he didn't move, I left the house, letting him sit there. This fellow then came everyday, wanting me to teach him German.

I said, "I am not a teacher" and left the house. But after a few days of this the Germans stopped talking as soon as I came along. They knew this *Kempeitai* person, and also knew that he came to my house. They ignored and avoided me like a leper.

Shortly afterwards, Shinichi came for a visit. He was permitted to move around. We in Hakone were not allowed to. I was still very agitated about the latest happenings, and told him that the *Kempeitai* wanted me to spy on the Germans. I have never seen Shinichi so angry. At once he wanted to go there to call them to account for their behaviour. Like me, he had never come across Japanese like that before. I had a VERY hard time stopping him and convincing him that I could handle it alone, even though I didn't know how. I was afraid what they would do to him; because I now knew that there is no justice, only power. What had become of that shy, timid girl who trustingly followed her love?

I guessed I was on the black list, and wondered what would happen to me if the war didn't end soon. But I would never give in to their machinations. One day, soon afterwards, that terrible fellow came again, saying I had to come to the Hakone hotel. I angrily asked why. He said there was a German lady who didn't speak enough Japanese and wanted me to translate for her. Secretly relieved that they didn't want to interrogate me on some trumped-up charges, I followed him. When we arrived at the hotel, there were two more *Kempeitai* sitting close to the entrance of the room. The lady for whom I was to translate was standing near them. An elderly, white-haired German lady, whom I also knew, was sitting Japanese style on the wooden floor on the other end. A chair for me was put in the middle. I was cautioned just to translate exactly what was said.

Now the trial examination began. The first lady (let me call her A), standing near the *Kempeitai*, was asked what the other had said to her. She answered that she hadn't understood it, because they were just passing each other on the street. The questioner was angry with this answer and asked again and again, but she stuck to it. Then he questioned the old lady. Eventually it came out that she had said, "Now the war will be over soon". ("Is that a crime", I wondered?) But the *Kempeitai* clenched his fists and struck her left and right in the face, so that she swayed from side to side. The first woman burst into tears, but I couldn't control my anger.

Springing up from the chair, with clenched fists in front of me I shouted, "HOW DARE YOU"!

He turned around, looking at me from head to toe and said smiling, "We don't need you anymore".

I knew I couldn't do anything and felt utterly helpless. The old whitehaired lady was never seen again. Why does war bring forth such cruelty in some people?

Chapter 7

After the War

Not long after that, the Emperor declared the end of the war. What a relief! Then followed the occupation by Americans (no fraternization). No one was allowed to leave Hakone without being screened by the occupation forces. Of course, they were busy with Tokyo, Yokohama and so on, and Hakone had to wait quite a while. All those who belonged to the *Partei* left. I don't know where they went. All others, including German women evacuees from Java, were asked whether they wanted to go to Germany. I was also asked, and they were astonished when I said I wanted to stay in Japan with my Japanese husband. If their experiences had been similar to mine it was no wonder they could not understand my decision.

But Shinichi Suzuki doesn't belong to one nation, he is just a wonderful human being and a true Christian, and lives according to the Commandments: "LOVE THY ENEMY" and "IF ONE STRIKES YOUR RIGHT CHEEK OFFER HIM YOUR LEFT". Because of him I still have faith in mankind. Yet, in the following years my faith was sometimes shaken again when I witnessed how people, not only Japanese, took advantage of Suzuki for their own ego and profit. And since those people cannot imagine a noble mind like Suzuki's, I am afraid they think he is silly, since he doesn't rebuke them, although he recognizes their bad behaviour and intentions.

The war was over, but not the problems. The Japanese currency was changed suddenly (I experienced that once before in Germany), and the new yen was frozen. That meant we were allowed to draw five hundred yen per month. That was enough for our rations, we were told. That happened while I was still in Hakone, and the Germans were just as dismayed as I was.

Suzuki had become very ill. He and the family had moved to Asama, a suburb of Matsumoto. Since he had given away all his meager rations, he himself had lived off the bark of trees. His stomach could no longer tolerate anything. He was just skin and bones, and he could not get up at all. His sister and the boys were still with him.

The question of survival of us all confronted me. Since I could now leave Hakone, I went to Yokohama, which was a shambles. Only a few big houses were standing. It was difficult to find my way around, because all the landmarks were gone. Finally I came to the small German school and went in. Various families were living there — Portuguese, English and one German lady with her 17-year-old daughter. She took me in for the night and begged me to accompany her daughter to the American Red Cross to ask for employment. She herself had a leg injury and couldn't go. While the girl was being interviewed, a Red Cross girl approached me, asking whether I would like to work there. I thought this was a gift from heaven and agreed, but first we had to see whether the provost marshal approved of us. He did and suggested that I work under my maiden name. As Suzuki I would only be paid like a Japanese. He gave me an ID card with the name: Joan Prange. Waltraud seemed to be too difficult to pronounce and Johanne is my middle name. So I started working at the information desk at the American Red Cross in 1945. The German lady occupied two rooms at the school, and she gave me the small one, since employment was not possible without living quarters.

Joan Prange [Waltraud Suzuki]
at the Red Cross Information Center.

I wanted to find lodgings so that Shinichi and I could live together again. I heard about a billeting office and went there. The officer in charge, an American first lieutenant, said if I found a house without a special mark on it, I could have it. During the little time I had, I wandered around. Luckily I found an unmarked little house, hidden from the main street; two rooms, kitchen and bath, not far from the German school. Right away I went to the billetting office to tell the officer about it. He asked for the exact location, made sure there was no mark on the house, and told me to come in again in a day or two. Busily planning to get Shinichi to move in with me, I went over the next day to look at 'my' house. Can you imagine my surprise, when I saw a colonel just coming out of the house, and in the process of locking it? I said, "What are you doing in my house?" He said it was just assigned to him by the billetting office, but offered me the key. Knowing I had lost, I didn't take the key, but went straight to the billetting office. There I confronted the officer, asking him the meaning of this dirty trick. Letting me find an unmarked house, promising it to me, and then giving it to someone else.

He said, "Do you think, I would do so much as this (snapping his fingers) for a German"?

In a loud, clear voice I said, "You gave your word. If a German officer gives his word, he keeps it, because his word is his honour". And then I added, full of contempt, "But YOU"! The room, where GIs were working, and also the connecting one with an open door, where a higher ranking officer was talking to someone, became deadly quiet.

The lieutenant said in a dangerously low voice, "I hope I never see you again in my life".

"That is mutual" I replied and left the room.

My trouble is that I always act impulsively, and only think later what could happen to me. Once again, the power was on the other side. But how can a single person like me account for the wrongdoings of a state? We met once again. The Red Cross messhall was connected with the officers' messhall, divided by a screen. We arrived at the same time at the entrance. In mocking irony, the lieutenant hurried to open the door wide for me, and smiling — with a bow, let me pass. But I noticed that he had been degraded from first to second lieutenant, and I believe that this was because of our encounter in his office.

Our money was still frozen. Inflation had driven the yen up to 360 to the dollar. I was paid ¥2,000 monthly, but since I had free lunch at the Red Cross messhall, I saved as much as I could and gave it to my sister-in-law, when I went to Asama on my free day. It was a grueling trip; standing for eight hours on a smoke-filled train.

Chapter 8

Working in Tokyo

Then one day a girl I hardly knew came to the Red Cross Information Center to ask me whether I would like to work in Tokyo with my salary to be paid in dollars. Of course, these were not real dollars, but scrip —little paper slips in a booklet marked one dollar each. With those, one could buy things at the OSS (Overseas Supply Store), like different food, not to be found in Japanese stores. I thought it would be wonderful, but I was not sure of myself. The girl told me she had found another, better paying job, but could not leave if there was no one to replace her. It was a shipping firm, based in Hong Kong. She talked me into having an interview with the boss, Mr. Morse. This interview was something to behold.

Mr. Morse, after a few preliminary remarks, asked, "Do you know anything about shipping documents"?

I had to be honest and replied, "I have never seen any".

"Well," said Mr. Morse, "can you type"?

"Yes, but very slowly", I had to answer.

"That will get better in time, won't it"? he asked.

"I guess so", was my reply. I thought that since I still had a job, I had better be VERY honest and not go into a new one under false pretenses or he might fire me when he learned the truth. Frankly, I was surprised when Mr. Morse said, "When can you start"?

My salary was fixed at 80 dollars. I had to give 14 days notice at the Red Cross, and then started at the new job in January, 1949. Besides Mr. Morse I was the only foreigner. The other employees were three Japanese men.

Office hours were from nine to five. For the first days after I started, Mr. Morse was present. Then he didn't come in for days. The Japanese knew that and took advantage of it. I was the only one there punctually at nine o'clock. On the second day of his absence Mr. Morse called exactly at nine. He wanted to speak to the Japanese manager. Reluctantly I had to admit that he was not yet in. Then he asked for some one else. I had to tell him that I was the only one in the office. So he wanted the manager to call him as soon as he came in. It was eleven o'clock when the manager finally came in!

I did my work, whether people were there or not and never left the office before five, even when I was through with my work before then. I locked the office and deposited the key downstairs.

One day, in a telephone conversation with a captain of the company's shipping line, Mr. Morse advised him to load cement at a particular port, because it was of better quality than that at an alternate port. The next morning, neither Mr. Morse nor any of the Japanese showed up. I answered the phone. It was the ship captain wanting to speak to Mr. Morse. When I told him Mr. Morse was not in just then, the captain said that there was no cement at the port recommended by Mr. Morse. He asked me what he should do? I had only been in that office about one and a half months and wondered myself what should he do.

But I thought, "Better a loaded ship then one going home empty", so I unhesitatingly told the captain to pick up the cement at the alternate port. Of course, the captain didn't know me, but he must have thought that I had authority because he did what I said. That night I couldn't sleep, worrying whether or not I had done the right thing. When Mr. Morse came in the next morning, I told him about the arrangement I had made. He didn't say anything, just nodded. So I still worried, thinking he didn't like it. But when I left the company, he gave me the following certificate:

TELEGRAPHIC ADD   MOLLERS TOKYO
ALL CODES:
TELEPHONE 24 4784

DIRECTORS
E B MOLLER
R B MOLLER
C B MOLLER
M M WATSON
D B EVANS

OUR REF   YOUR REF

HEAD OFFICE
HONGKONG
ASSOCIATED
COMPANIES AT:
CALCUTTA
DURBAN
LONDON
NEW YORK
SHANGHAI
SINGAPORE

MOLLERS' LIMITED

(INCORPORATED IN HONGKONG)
JAPAN BRANCH
ROOM 409
TOKYO HOTEL
TOKYO

July 16, 1949

TO WHOM IT MAY CONCERN

This is to certify that Miss Joan
Prange was employed by this company from 4-1-49
to 15/6/49 in the capacity of typist, mailing,
filing and cabling clerk during which period
we found her to be most diligent, punctual, and
attentive to her duties which she discharged to
our entire satisfaction at all times. She like-
wise showed initiative to a degree where we
were relieved of routine shipping matters which
Miss Prange was able to control without reference
to the management. Her services were terminated
due to closure of our office and we do not
hesitate in recommending her to a company de-
siring a clerk in the capacity referred to.

MOLLERS LTD.

R. G. MORSE
Japan Representative

RGM/an

Recommendation Letter from Mollers' Limited

Only then, did I know I had done the right thing.

Working in Tokyo.

Six months after I started working there, the company closed down. Mr. Morse told me not to worry because he would find a job for me. He recommended me to the Chartered Bank, where he was a customer. He told me the personnel manager would like to see me. I was frightened, knowing nothing of banking. Yet, even though I knew I must work because I had to make a living for my sick husband and his sister, who took care of him, I didn't go to the bank until I received a letter from the personnel manager of the bank, asking me to come and see him. I wondered what Mr. Morse had told him, because he wrote such a nice letter. He would indeed be very pleased if I joined the Chartered Bank. So I finally went for an interview, and was employed for 100 dollars a month.

One of the girls working there had a Japanese mother and an English father. She was supposed to instruct me, but she told me nothing. Somehow she had found out that

I got a higher salary than she did. She went to the personnel manager to complain because a newcomer, who knew nothing, was to be paid more than she. I guess he told her that that was for the management to decide. She said in that case she would quit, probably hoping that he would not let her go. But she was mistaken, and so she quit. I only found out the reason later, and only then did I understand WHY she was so hostile to me.

Since she hadn't told me anything in a few days we were together, I felt rather helpless. My superior, Mr. Graham, was very nice about it and told me to look up former correspondence to acquaint myself with the work, or to ask him.

I could hardly finish all the work. Blaming myself for being too slow, I stayed on after five, usually till about eight o'clock. The English officers did the same. But one day, Mr. Graham again dumped a load of work on my desk. I looked the stack over and realized that this work didn't belong in my category. So I took it straight back to him saying, "That is YOUR work, so please do it yourself". He laughed and said, "So you finally caught on". No wonder I could never finish my work. But on Saturdays I always left punctually at one to catch the train to Matsumoto.

Becky, the English secretary, invited me several times to go with her to the English Club to watch cricket, but I always declined. She asked what I did at weekends? So finally I told her my reason for always going to Matsumoto, but begged her to keep it secret. Once, during my visit to my husband, Hina, my sister-in-law, said the doctor had given him up. I wanted to stay with him, but Hina said, "You are the only breadwinner, if you give up your job, we will all starve". Sick at heart, I went back to Tokyo, crying and praying all the way. Shortly after, the miracle happened, Suzuki got better, and finally he could get up. After a while they moved into a house in Matsumoto and slowly, little by little, Shinichi started teaching again. Then he urged me to come home.

Matsumoto Castle

But before I resigned, new worries were to come. Shinichi, visiting me in Tokyo, told me that his landlord had to sell the house, and had offered it to him for one million yen. Of course, such a sum was unthinkable for us. Suzuki found and moved into another one with a small down-payment and monthly installments for 20 years. When I came next to Matsumoto, Shinichi was very depressed, saying that the violin didn't sound well in this typical Japanese house with low ceilings and tatami floors. And it was too small for teaching. I called a carpenter and the three of us made plans for a big western style room with a high ceiling. There Shinichi could teach again, and Talent Education started anew after the war. But it meant that I still had to keep on working. When the addition to the house had been paid for and some furniture bought I finally left the bank in 1956 after five and a half years working there, and went home. Suzuki didn't want to live in Tokyo again, so Matsumoto became 'home'.

Years later we gradually enlarged and changed the house. There is not much left from the original purchase. One of the rooms was used as an office. Mr. Shida, Tomiko's father, and one mother worked there. Tomiko Shida is one of the three Matsumoto girls who started lessons there with Suzuki. In the beginning they had to share one violin among them. Tomiko Shida-Lauwers now lives in Brussels. She formed a Quartet (de l'Opera National de Belgique) and concertizes.

Matsumoto, The Original House

**The house with a western style room built on.
Outside view.**

Here was where the addition was built on.

Before settling down in Matsumoto I wanted to go to
Germany to see my relatives and friends, since I had not
been there since 1928. With Shinichi's agreement, I used the
bonus which I had received from the bank when I left, for this
purpose.

Chapter 9

A Visit to Europe

Musicians in Greece had heard about the musical education of small children and had begged by letter for more information. I wrote to them that I would make a stopover in Athens on my way back from Germany to Japan to see them. They awaited me at the airport, and we talked until late into the night. They wouldn't hear about my staying at a hotel (which I had already booked in Germany) but offered me their hospitality. I spent four days with this nice family, who had two children. Besides explaining Talent Education, there was sightseeing which included the Acropolis and a boat-trip.

Prof. Scuisis and Family, Athens

From Athens, Istanbul is "right around the corner". Thinking I would never have the occasion again to be so near, I wanted to have a look. So off I went. I took a guided tour together with other people along the Bosporus, and on another day went to the Bazaar and the Blue Mosque. Unforgettable impressions.

Chapter 10

Talent Education

Back in Japan there was now only Shinichi's income to count on. We still had to be very careful about spending money. But gradually our livelihood improved. Our home was the school. Students came from morning to evening. On Fridays the *Kenkyuseis* (teacher trainees) came in the morning for lessons, had lunch with us, lessons again, the tea before they left. It was a busy time. Perhaps it was too much for Suzuki. One day he nearly doubled up with pain after just a little bite. This happened whenever he tried to eat anything. I was terribly worried. Was it cancer of the stomach? For three days he refused to eat anything and he didn't want to see a doctor. I cooked a gruel of oatmeal for him, but he didn't want to eat it. I insisted, saying that even babies could tolerate it. Slowly he started to eat, and finished the whole plate. He was so happy and said, "No pain". This was his diet from then on for nearly three years. Gradually, very gradually I added milk, honey, egg yoke and wheat germ. Suzuki was still on this diet when Mr. John Kendall came to Japan in 1959 to observe Talent Education. He had seen a film of our annual concert, taken in 1956, which Mr. Kenji Mochizuki introduced in 1958 to Clifford Cook at Oberlin College in Ohio. Having a sabbatical leave, Mr. Kendall was curious to see where those small children learned to play the violin so beautifully. After the Second World War there was a world-wide shortage of good stringed instrument players.

Later the famous cellist Pablo Casals came to Tokyo in 1961 to attend a Suzuki children's concert in his honor. He was very moved after listening to the children, and when

Suzuki came to him to thank him for coming, he threw his arms around him and wept on his shoulder.

Pablo Casals at Tokyo Concert

The maestro went on stage and gave the following speech:
> "Ladies and gentlemen, I assist to one
> of the most moving scenes, that one
> can see. What we are contemplating
> has much more importance than it seems,
> I don't think that in any country in
> the world we could feel such spirit of
> fraternity or cordiality in its utmost.
> I feel in every moment that I have had
> of living in this country such proof of
> heart, of desire of a better world.
> And this is what has impressed me most
> in this country. The superlative desire
> of highest things in life and how
> wonderful it is to see that the grown-
> up people think of the smallest like
> this as to teach them to begin with the
> noble feelings, with noble deeds. And
> one of these is music. To train them to

music to make them understand that
music is not only sound to have to dance
or to have small pleasure, but such
high thing in life that perhaps it is
music that will save the world.
Now, I not only congratulate you, the
teachers, the grown-up people, but I
want to say: my whole respect and my
heartiest congratulations. And another
thing I am happy to say at this moment
is that Japan is a great people, and
Japan is not only great by its deeds
in industry, in science, in art, but
Japan is, I would say, the heart of the
heart, and this is what humanity needs
first, first, first".

Casals in Tokyo, 1961

Between the 1955 annual concert and 1963 many American teachers came to Matsumoto to study and observe. Mr. & Mrs. Corina were among the first. Mrs. Corina is now a well-known Suzuki violin teacher in California, and has visited Matsumoto nine times. She came to Tokyo again for Suzuki's 88th birthday party in 1986. Professor Clifford Cook from Oberlin College came in 1962. And, of course, Mr. Kendall returned several times. It was decided that we, together with ten Suzuki children and some teachers, should come to the United States for a concert tour. This happened in 1964 and was an overwhelming success. From then on Suzuki and I were invited to come to the states every year during the summer months. Suzuki demonstrated, taught and lectured. His English was not too good at the time, so during intermissions people would crowd around me, asking what he had said and meant. We went to different locations every year, mostly for two weeks at any one place.

In Japan, of course, teaching went on as before. But very often now, little children came to our house in the evenings with their mothers to play at home concerts for foreign observers. However, we have had a school building — the *Kaikan* — for more than ten years. It was built by private funds: from mothers, teachers, and, of course, Suzuki. The funds from mothers had to be given back after two years. All others donated monthly. This was again a difficult time. Now our house is quiet.

But there was no one in the office who spoke English. So all foreign correspondence became my responsibility. Europe, South America and Africa heard about the tremendous success of the Suzuki Method. That brought more visitors and more mail. Finally we had an English speaking girl in the office who could handle part of the mail.

Chapter 11

"Nurtured By Love"

People started asking why Suzuki didn't write a book so everyone could understand his philosophy better. He wrote one, but in Japanese. Then everyone demanded that it be translated. That was easier said than done. I asked Mr. Mochizuki to do it, but after six months when I asked how he was getting on, he said it was too difficult and that he couldn't do it. I next asked Dr. Honda, who said he had tried it and found it too difficult to translate. I suggested to Suzuki that we have a professional translator do it, but he feared the result would be too cold and impersonal. As the clamour for a translation grew I thought, "Well, I'll just have to try it—there is no alternative."

From early in the morning till late at night I worked on the translation. One day Suzuki asked me, "What are you doing so early in the morning and so late at night every day"?

"I am trying to translate your book", I answered.

"You?! Every one says it is too difficult". Suzuki said with a smile, probably thinking I would give up, too.

That made me answer, "That is why I am doing it"!

Well, then I was committed, but there certainly were times when I *wanted* to give it up, because it WAS so difficult. My husband always says, if one is determined, one will succeed, so I doggedly kept on. When I finished, six months later, I never wanted to see a another *Kanji*[1] again, but I wanted to have the book printed and ready before we went to the United States in May. I called our American

---

[1]*Kanji* , Chinese character

publisher from California and asked him to send about 100 copies of the book to each of the locations to which we were going. *Nurtured by Love* sold like hot cakes.

After the book was out, the new education method spread rapidly. My translation was fruitful in another way some years later.

Chapter 12

Dr. Suzuki Receives Recognition

In 1977, an American businessman in his late thirties read it and was so impressed that he wanted to meet the author. He came to Matsumoto and talked to Shinichi, asking for his further plans. Of course, Suzuki had those. He had already talked with an architect about plans for another building. The Kaikan was just paid for, and I was not too happy thinking of the immense costs for another one. But when Suzuki talked to Mr. David Smith about a new research center, he inquired about the costs, and said, "Go ahead and build it, I will pay for it". Shinichi just said:, "Thank you" as if he were offered a cup of coffee or a cigarette. So I asked my husband, in Japanese, "Did you hear what he said"? Calmly he answered, "Yes, he wants to pay for the building". I was shocked. Why would a stranger give away so much money? So I asked Mr. Smith, "Why are you doing this"? He said, "Well, so far I have always thought of making money. Now I have enough and want to do some good, to help people like Mr. Suzuki". I still wasn't satisfied and said, "What do you want out of it"? He said, "Nothing". In this way the problem of the new building was solved. And secretly I was proud that my translation brought this about. We were shocked to hear some years later that Mr. Smith died as the result of an accident in Italy.

Kaikan

**Suzuki's Birthday in the Kaikan
after its completion.**

New Building: Suzuki Method Institute

Going through the mail at the Kaikan.

Chapter 13

More Travels

Twice I went to Germany privately. Once I returned by plane, making a stop over at New Delhi, where a German couple had invited me. During the three days there, I visited the Taj Mahal in Agra, and will never forget it. The next time, I took a Dutch freighter with only 12 passengers on board. We docked at Cairo, Egypt, but the captain would not allow us to go on land, because he wanted to leave again soon since the ship was already late. We were dismayed. But then, in the Suez Canal, the engine broke down. As the captain had to stay there for two days to let all other ships pass (the Suez Canal is small, there is only one way passage) we finally could return to Cairo. All the passengers were jubilant. Our passports were taken away and we were allowed to explore Cairo with a guide. We were taken to the museum, admired king Tut-anch-Amon's inner sarcophagus of pure gold, and all the other fabulous treasures kept there, and saw some ancient preserved mummies and much more. On the next day I went with two other passengers on a camel ride to the desert to admire the pyramids and the Sphinx. Then the ship took us to Singapore.

Becky, whom I mentioned earlier, had married and was now living in Singapore, where her husband (whom I also knew from my Chartered Bank days) was working with the same bank. Becky was waiting for me at the harbour, and I stayed at their house. She showed me around Singapore. We had a look at the strange custom of "Death-houses", where they take people to die. We had a very nice time together until my ship finally left. We were in Singapore for five days though.

In order to board the ship, I had to show my passport to a guard quite a distance from the ship itself. He looked at it, and looked at it. I wondered whether he couldn't read. So finally I asked, "Is there something wrong"? He said, still in deep thoughts, "You were beautiful". PAST tense, mind you!! I had to laugh.

This is the passport photograph in question.

Then we went to Bangkok, a fascinating place I had always wanted to see. There we had only two days, but I saw the famous Floating Market, the Golden Buddha and the palace. In Bangkok too, officers from the Chartered Bank, whom I knew from Tokyo, helped me.

When we finally docked in Yokohama, I got a letter which my husband had left with the port office, saying that he had come twice to greet me on my return, but the ship had not arrived at the time I gave him, and that he really could not come a third time.(I didn't blame him). But because of all the delay, I had a wonderful trip.

The first European tour of the Suzuki children was arranged in 1970. I went along to translate and explain in Berlin. The group then went to London, while I went to Munich to visit Professor Klingler who was ill. He died about two months later. I met the group again in Lisbon, and then we went to the U.S.. I also went with the Suzuki tour group to Peru in 1979, where the highly cultured Inca lived several hundred years ago, In 1983 we visited China - Shanghai, Xian and Beijing, VERY fascinating. The name Suzuki is well known in China and we, the teachers, and the American and Japanese Suzuki children had VIP treatment all the way.

In Xian we were overwhelmed at the sight of the terra cotta army, livesize with their horses. It was the most fantastic sight. The long way to the emperor's tomb is flanked by massive sculptured lions, winged horses, *etc.* Another MUST was to climb the Great Wall, and I have a medal to prove it. And, of course, we had a look at the fabulous Forbidden City. Two weeks are just not enough for China.

For our Golden Wedding anniversary in 1978 a festival in a Tokyo hotel was prepared for us with about 600 persons present. Shinichi asked me, "When is the next big anniversary"? I skipped the 60th and said, "Oh, 25 years from now". He calculated how old he would be then; I laughed and said, "I won't be around anymore". He looked at me and said wonderingly, "You don't want to go before that, do you"? My niece and nephew with their spouses came from America for the celebration. They invited us afterwards for a trip to Hong Kong, Bali, Penang and Singapore. Shinichi did not go, but I did and enjoyed it immensely.

50th Wedding Anniversary.

Yes, I have travelled around quite a bit in our beautiful world and loved it. Talent Education and the Suzuki Method have grown, and I am still busy and travel around with Suzuki to workshops because he cannot go alone. But now, we go every year to a different country in Europe too, besides America and Australia.

I don't mind that at all. The bad side of the coin is that whenever trouble occurs, I have to deal with it. Who else? Suzuki is VERY busy and needs his strength for his

Australia, October 1978.

Australia, October 1978.

work. I don't want him to be bothered with time consuming unpleasant things. And I try to protect him from people, who want to gain financially by his name or otherwise to boost their own egos. It is really sad, that there are always individuals who want to take advantage of him. When Suzuki founded the I.S.A. (International Suzuki Association.) in 1984 and I was elected vice-president, I had to endure the hostility of different people. But those people didn't seem to realize that I have been doing the same work for years without any title, which I do not covet, as some others obviously do.

Many foreign teacher trainees come to Matsumoto. I try to help them when they encounter problems. But even keeping fairly busy, I sometimes feel very lonely. My mother died several years ago (1976) at the age of 98, in America where she had lived with my widowed sister and her children. A requiem mass was held for her in our Matsumoto church. My sister has had two strokes and is not well.

In Matsumoto, I had one good friend, a Japanese lady. She too died some years ago. My very good friends in Germany are deceased also. Suzuki, who was a wonderful conversationalist, is now completely wrapped up in his work. There is so much more he wants to do besides music education. He wants to change the public school education, and tried it already some 25 years ago with a primary class for five years with tremendous success. However, this is all described in *Nurtured by Love* so I don't have to go into it here.

In June 1986 I spent a week at the house of Henry and Anne Turner, who are good friends of ours. Henry is retired and Anne an excellent Suzuki piano teacher. David, their handsome son, and two lovely daughters complete the nice family. Oh, I forgot Mary, their Irish setter guard dog, who never barks. It is always very enjoyable for me to stay with them. At the Turner's home in Little Abbotsbury I met Becky again. She had kept in touch with me in all those years through occasional correspondence, and as she now lives in London, she came to see me.

Henry and Anne escorted me to Tetbury, Gloustershire, where I, some teachers, and the Suzuki children had the honour to meet Princess Diana of Wales at a charity concert given by the Suzuki children.

Princess Diana of Wales in Tetburg, 1986.

For Suzuki's 88th birthday in October 1986 some lovely parties were held (88 is a special year in Japan). One party was held by the city of Matsumoto. The Mayor of Matsumoto gave the following speech:

Heartfelt Congratulations.
Shohjia   wago
Mayor of Matsumoto
    Mr. Suzuki was born on October 17, 1898, and he turns eighty-eight years old this month in great health.
    For us, he is a teacher, or a father -- indeed a presence we should call a paternal mentor. I thought it would be great to celebrate his *BEIJU*[2] birthday together, and took the liberty to initiate the project. That is why those who love and admire him are here, so many of us, in honor of this particularly felicitous day.
    Thank you, Mr. Suzuki, for coming today. All 200,000 Matsumoto citizens, as well as those of us who have gathered here, congratulate you on your eighty-eighth anniversary. Felicitations.
    I need not describe his work as a musician and educator, for it is widely recognized in society and applauded throughout the world. It is no exaggeration to say that we in Matsumoto have Matsumoto Castle, a national treasure, to show the world.
    There is a saying which goes, "the crab digs a hole the size of its shell". We ordinary mortals tend to measure things by our own yardsticks. Yet there are things in the world far beyond the scope of regular yardsticks, and there are also individuals far beyond such scope.
    I often have a chance to see Mr. Suzuki, although usually it is no more than a brief, business-only contact. On those occasions I always find it strange, though is may be

---

[2]*Beiju* , the celebration of the rice year, means age eighty-eight or the eighty-eighth birthday, because the three Chinese characters for eighty-eight share the same six strokes as the character *bei* , rice.

impolite to say so, that somehow I don't feel as if I am talking with a musician; nor do I feel that he is an educator.

It is as if I am talking with someone beyond the ordinary yardstick that defines a musician or an educator, someone deeper and warmer, perhaps comparable to a god or the Kannon —honestly, this is my feeling.

'Man is a child of his environment' is a beautiful proverb which is at the heart of the Suzuki Method. It can be said of Mr. Suzuki himself. At the crucial stage of his human formation, he came into close contact with Marquis Yoshichika Tokugawa of the former Owari Province, Einstein, Professor Klingler, and, through them, many other leading individuals of the time. He struggled hard in his work during and after the war. He fell ill and wandered near death. Through these truly great friendships, rare experiences, and varied environments, Mr. Suzuki must have grown greater, deeper and warmer. This is one way I view the proverb.

As in the darkness right under a lighthouse, I am afraid we remain unenlightened as to Mr. Suzuki's height, greatness and depth even as we are always near him.

As you know, Newton discovered the law of gravity when watching an apple fall. Mr. Suzuki discovered the law of ability when listening to young children's conversation. In that each sensitively grasped a great law of the universe or of mankind. I think they represent two peaks in the East and West.

'The Law of Ability' which Mr. Suzuki discovered has developed into the Suzuki Method, spread throughout the world, and is fostering more outstanding children than the number of his favorite twinkling stars.

We, especially postwar Japanese, tend to emphasize the visible, or things, and neglect to invisible but crucial values: questions of inner human ability, talent, and mankind's future potential.

Matsumoto citizens who in the past founded Kaichi School and Matsumoto High School can now take pride in Mr. Suzuki's Talent Education Institute. This is happiness we cannot exchange for anything else. I renew my sincere respect and gratitude toward Mr. Suzuki's great work, which has enriched us visibly and invisibly, especially by implanting in us Matsumoto citizens a global, or international sense.

Mr. Suzuki has often said, 'My retirement age is one-hundred and ten'. It may perhaps be impolite to celebrate his birthday when he is only eighty-eight. However, I hope he will accept our small but heartfelt congratulations. May he and Mrs. Suzuki stay healthy and youthful as ever, and guide us long. Congratulations, Mr. Suzuki.

Then the Matsumoto teachers, followed by all *Kenkyuseis* (teachers in training), the Kindergarten and later the office staff held a party for him. In November a party was arranged at a Tokyo hotel with eight hundred well wishers. And in December there was a concert at the Suntory Hall, where his very early pupils played for him. There were 2000 guests.

The Eighth International Suzuki Conference is being held in West Berlin in 1987. Shinichi and I are looking forward to it with great expectations. Suzuki studied there as an unknown student. Now he comes back as a world famous professor to the city he loves, and which holds some of the most wonderful memories of our lives.

Chapter 14

Conclusion

In these times of juvenile delinquency and drug abuse the Suzuki philosophy could be a guidance for a better world. The Suzuki Method brings family unity, and we should take to heart his words:

"If love is deep, much can be accomplished".

Chapter 15

Awards and Honours

**Suzuki's 88th birthday party, Tokyo, 1986.
Attended by about 800 people.**

During recent years Suzuki has received many honours and decorations.

Degrees
Honorary Doctorates of Music

New England Conservatory	1966
University of Louisville	1967
Eastman School of Music, University of Rochester	1972
Oberlin College	1984

Honorary Distinguished Professor

North East Louisiana University	1982

Awards

Chunichi Newspapers Culture Award	1951
Shinmai Newspapers Culture Award	1961
Ysaye Award (Belgium)	1969
Order of the Sacred Treasure, Third Class	1970
Mobile Music Award	1976
Palmes Academiques (France)	1982
The Japan Foundation Award	1983
Des Bundesverdienstkreuz 1. Klasse (West Germany)	1985
Omaggio a Venezia from L'associazion "Omaggio a Venezia" (Italy)	1985

Honorary Citizenships

Winnipeg, Alberta, Canada	1972
Atlanta, Georgia, U.S.A.	1978
Matsumoto, Nagano-ken, Japan	1979
Monroe, Louisiana, U.S.A.	1982

Other Information
Honorary member of Rotary Club Matsumoto, and Paul Harris Fellow of Rotary International.

Honorary Citizenship, Matsumoto.

**Honorary Citizenship
(Festival), Matsumoto**

Ysaye Award, Belgium.

Palmes Academiques, France.

**Des Bundesverdienstkreuz
1. Klasse, West Germany.**